BiRDS

Carme Lemniscates

CANDLEWICK STUDIO
an imprint of Candlewick Press

Birds come in many different colors, shapes, and personalities.

Some birds are really big.

Others are tiny.

Some like to show off, while others would rather watch.

Some birds are very noisy.
Others sing a sweet and tender song.

Some like to go on long journeys.
Others like to stay cozy at home.

Most like to build nests
from branches.

Some prefer a roof over their head.

But no matter what, nearly all like to have conversations.

Tweet, tweet! calls one.

Cheep, cheep! replies another.

For every call, there is a response.

A bird's song is like
the loving words of a friend.

A happy song that greets us every morning.

And our hearts sing, too, because birds are like good news coming.

Or messages of peace.

Birds are like thoughts.
They come, stay awhile . . .

and then fly away.

They fly where their hearts call them.

Birds are free.

They make our imaginations soar.

Library of Congress Catalog Card Number pending. ISBN 978-1-5362-0178-9. This book was typeset in Lunchbox. The illustrations were done in mixed media.

Candlewick Studio, an imprint of Candlewick Press, 99 Dover Street, Somerville, Massachusetts 02144. www.candlewickstudio.com.

Printed in Heshan, Guangdong, China 18 19 20 21 22 23 LEO 10 9 8 7 6 5 4 3 2 1